YOU M ___ ___ THIS

1953

MILESTONES, MEMORIES,
TRIVIA AND FACTS, NEWS EVENTS,
PROMINENT PERSONALITIES &
SPORTS HIGHLIGHTS OF THE YEAR

TO : Glenn

FROM : Bettina

MESSAGE : Happiest birthday ever.
You were the best thing to happen in
1953!

*selected and researched
by
mary a. pradt*

WARNER **W** TREASURES ™

PUBLISHED BY WARNER BOOKS

A TIME WARNER COMPANY

Warner Books, Inc.
1271 Avenue of the Americas
New York, New York 10020

Warner Treasures is a
trademark of Warner Books, Inc.

W A Time Warner Company

DESIGN:
CAROL BOKUNIEWICZ DESIGN
PRINTED IN SINGAPORE
FIRST PRINTING : MAY 1995
10 9 8 7 6 5 4 3 2 1
ISBN : 0-446-91029-5

dwight d. eisenhower took the oath of office January 20. His was the first Republican administration in 24 years. Ike had promised to "clean up the mess" in Washington and to end the stalemate in Korea. He was aided at first in his relations with Congress by Senator Robert A. Taft, but Taft died July 31 and was replaced by a Democrat in the Senate. Vice President Nixon was President of the Senate. When Chief Justice Fred Vinson died in September, Eisenhower got to appoint California's Governor Earl Warren to the high court, where Warren's impact proved monumental.

julius and ethel rosenberg, the convicted atomic spies, were executed June 19, in the electric chair. They were the first husband and wife to receive the ultimate punishment.

A VACCINE AGAINST POLIO WAS TESTED SUCCESSFULLY, DR. JONAS SALK REPORTED IN MARCH. MORE TESTS WOULD BE NEEDED TO DETERMINE THE EFFECTIVENESS AND SAFETY OF THE VACCINE.

newsreel

Senator Joe McCarthy continued his tirades. He assailed the outgoing administration for being lax and the incoming one for timidity. He attacked the "Voice of America" broadcasts and spearheaded an inquiry into an alleged spy network in a New Jersey army signal corps lab. McCarthy also pursued the overseas libraries of the State Department, to root out subversion. On June 17, at Dartmouth, Eisenhower condemned "book burners."

joseph stalin,

the Soviet leader, succumbed to a stroke in Moscow, in March, at 73. He had been a ruthless leader responsible for millions of deaths and disappearances.

headlines

John Foster Dulles warned of a possible "domino effect" in Southeast Asia, if the French should fail to defeat the Viet Minh and Communism in Indochina. French paratroopers landed at Dien Bien Phu November 29. Ho Chi Minh, the Communist leader, predicted that Americans would come to replace French troops eventually.

As repatriation after the Korean War began, 23 American POWs and one Brit refused to return home. Some 27,000 North Korean prisoners of war also refused to be repatriated.

IN JUNE, MOUN-
TAINEER EDMUND
HILLARY AND TENZIG
NORKAY, HIS SHERPA
GUIDE, BECAME THE
FIRST TO CONQUER
MOUNT EVEREST.

queen elizabeth II

was crowned with much ceremony in Westminster Abbey June 2. Attendees included heads of state from India, Pakistan, Australia, New Zealand, and South Africa. Sultans came from Zanzibar and Brunei. Prince Charles, four, and Princess Anne, two, received lots of attention and got restless and cranky.

5

University of Iowa scientists announced in December that they had achieved the first human pregnancies using

deep-frozen sperm

STUDIES SHOWED THAT BETTER-OFF RESIDENTS OF NEW YORK AND OTHER LARGE CITIES ARE MOVING IN GREAT NUMBERS TO THE SUBURBS. CITIES MUST MAKE THEIR IMAGE MORE ATTRACTIVE, CREATE MORE LIGHT AND AIRY SPACES, AND REEMPHASIZE THEIR ADVANTAGES, ADVISED PLANNERS.

jane russell and marilyn monroe starred in the film version of *Gentlemen Prefer Blondes.*

GENERAL GEORGE C. MARSHALL WAS AWARDED THE NOBEL PEACE PRIZE, AND **WINSTON CHURCHILL** WON THE NOBEL PRIZE IN LITERATURE.

cultural
milestones

American tourist travel was up 13 percent over 1951, according to the American Automobile Association. Western national parks and the southwest in general were becoming popular. The AAA recommended a vacation budget for two persons of $27 a day, allowing $8 for accommodations, $8 for meals, and $2 for admissions, amusements, and tolls. This would come to about $210 for a week vacation for two, about $400 for two weeks.

OZZIE AND HARRIET, RICKY, AND DAVID NELSON were our favorite TV family, Fridays at 8:00 P.M.

FOR THE KIDS—"THE PINKY LEE SHOW" FEATURED THE FORMER PINCUS LEFF, WHO GOT HIS START IN VAUDEVILLE. PINKY WORE A TWEED CHECKERED COAT, MATCHING BAGGY PANTS, AND A PORKPIE HAT. KIDS LOVED HIM, MONDAYS THROUGH SATURDAYS AT 10:00 A.M. ON NBC.

television

There were 20.4 million TV households in America; the percentage of homes with TV had reached 44.7.

top rated tv shows
of the 1953–54 season:

1. "I Love Lucy" (CBS)

2. "Dragnet" (NBC)

3. "Arthur Godfrey's Talent Scouts" (CBS)

4. "You Bet Your Life" — Groucho Marx (NBC)

5. "The Chevy Show" — Bob Hope (NBC)

6. "The Milton Berle Show" (NBC)

7. "Arthur Godfrey and His Friends" (CBS)

8. "The Ford Show" (NBC)

9. "The Jackie Gleason Show" (CBS)

10. "Fireside Theater" (NBC)

11. "The Colgate Comedy Hour" (NBC)

12. "This Is Your Life" (NBC)

13. "The Red Buttons Show" (CBS)

14. "The Life of Riley" (NBC)

15. "Our Miss Brooks" (CBS)

color tv

was about to become a reality. Bizet's opera *Carmen* was broadcast in color on NBC October 31. It could also be received on monochrome sets. NBC also broadcast "Kukla, Fran, and Ollie" with the Boston Pops in color. A minuscule fraction of 1 percent of Americans had color sets, but they would flood the stores by the holiday shopping season.

The wedding of the decade, actually, was that of **SENATOR JOHN F. KENNEDY,** a Harvard graduate and wartime PT-boat commander, to **JACQUELINE LEE BOUVIER,** in Newport, RI, September 12. The new Mrs. Kennedy had recently worked as the inquiring photographer of the *Washington Times-Herald*.

celeb wedding of the year

milestones

DEATHS

Robert Taft,
Ohio Senator, died of cancer July 31. Up to the end, he was Ike's strongest ally in Congress.

Maude Adams,
the famous actress who originated the Peter Pan role on the American stage in 1905, died July 17. She performed the role more than 1,500 times, as well as playing many Shakespearean roles.

Dowager Queen Mary,
widow of King George V, mother of two kings and grandmother of Queen Elizabeth II, died March 24; she would have been 86 May 26.

Sergei Prokofiev,
Russian composer best known for *The Love for Three Oranges* and, in a lighter vein, *Peter and the Wolf*, died March 8 in Moscow.

Jim Thorpe,
the American Indian all-around athlete who won the 1912 Olympics for the U.S. almost singlehandedly but was stripped of his medals because he had played pro baseball, died at 64 March 28.

William Tatem Tilden,
who was named the greatest tennis player of the first half of the century, died in Hollywood June 5.

births

KIM BASINGER, film star, was born in Athens, GA, December 8.

AMY IRVING, actress, was born in Palo Alto September 10.

JOANNA KERNS, actress, was born February 12.

KAY LENZ, actress and former wife of David Cassidy, was born March 4, in Los Angeles.

ALFRE WOODARD, black actress, was born in Tulsa November 2.

ROSEANNE (BARR) ARNOLD, comedian, was born in Salt Lake City November 3.

GRETE WAITZ, track athlete, was born October 1.

KEITH HERNANDEZ, baseball player, was born in San Francisco October 20.

TITO JACKSON, singer and member of the Jackson 5, was born in Gary, IN, October 15.

PAT BENATAR (PATRICIA ANDREJEWSKI), rock star, was born in Brooklyn January 10.

DESI ARNAZ, JR., actor, was born January 19.

KEN BURNS, producer, director, cinematographer, and writer best known for "The Civil War," was born July 29.

CHRISTIE BRINKLEY, supermodel, was born February 2 in L.A.

MARY STEENBURGEN, actress from Arkansas, was born in 1953, all sources agree—but no one's identified the date.

top pop singles

53

1. **song from moulin rouge**
   percy faith

2. **vaya con dios**
   les paul and mary ford

3. **doggie in the window**
   patti page

4. **i'm walking behind you**
   eddie fisher

5. **you, you, you**
   ames brothers

6. **till i waltz again with you**
   teresa brewer

7. **april in portugal**
   les baxter

8. **no other love**
   perry como

9. **don't let the stars get in your eyes**
   perry como

10. **i believe**
    frankie laine

hit music

top pop LPs

1. **music for lovers only**
   jackie gleason

2. **hans christian andersen**
   danny kaye

3. **stars and stripes forever**
   alfred newman

4. **music of victor herbert**
   mantovani

5. **kay starr style**
   kay starr

6. **south pacific**
   original cast

7. **i'm in the mood for love**
   eddie fisher

8. **bye bye blues**
   les paul and mary ford

9. **by the light of the silvery moon**
   doris day

10. **call me madam**
    ethel merman and others

Perry Como

top R&B singles

1. **(mama) he treats your daughter mean**
   ruth brown

2. **shake a hand**
   faye adams

3. **hound dog**
   willie mae thornton

4. **crying in the chapel**
   orioles

5. **the clock**
   johnny ace

6. **i don't know**
   willie mabon

7. **good lovin'**
   clovers

8. **baby, don't do it**
   five royales

9. **help me somebody**
   five royales

10. **please love me**
    b. b. king

ALSO ON THE R&B CHARTS WERE NUMBERS BY CLYDE
MCPHATTER, FATS DOMINO, AND THE DU DROPPERS.

fiction

1. **the robe**
   lloyd c. douglas

2. **the silver chalice**
   thomas b. costain

3. **desiree**
   annemarie selinko

4. **battle cry**
   leon uris

5. **from here to eternity**
   james jones

6. **the high and the mighty**
   ernest k. gann

7. **beyond this place**
   a. j. cronin

8. **time and time again**
   james hilton

9. **lord vanity**
   samuel shellabarger

10. **the unconquered**
    ben ames williams

bestselling

14

nonfiction

1. **the holy bible:
   revised standard version**

2. **the power of
   positive thinking**
   norman vincent peale

3. **sexual behavior in
   the human female**
   alfred c. kinsey
   and others.

4. **angel unaware**
   dale evans rogers

5. **life is worth living**
   fulton j. sheen

6. **a man called peter**
   catherine marshall

7. **this i believe**
   ed. by edward p. morgan

8. **the greatest faith
   ever known**
   fulton oursler and
   g.a.o. armstrong

9. **how to play your
   best golf**
   tommy armour

10. **a house is not a home**
    polly adler

books

YES, that last entry is the memoir of a famous madam, right in there with all the religious and inspirational stuff people were reading. Of course, that Kinsey report sold briskly, too.

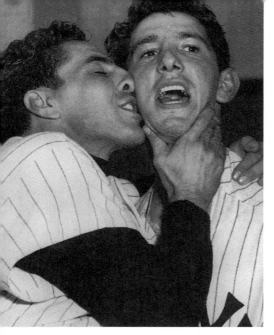

the biggest sports story of the year

was the Yankees' rewriting the record book by winning their *fifth* series in a row, under the guidance of Casey Stengel. The Yankee pennant victory in the American League and their success over the Brooklyn Dodgers put the Yanks and Stengel in a class of their own. It was the first time in major league history a club and a manager had won five successive pennants and series.

Maureen Connolly of San Diego extended her reign as the world's best woman tennis player and added the distinction of being the first woman to win the Australian, French, Wimbledon, and U.S. titles.

THE INDIANA HOOSIERS AND SETON HALL WERE COLLEGIATE LEADERS. SETON HALL SET A MAJOR COLLEGE RECORD BY WINNING 27 CONSECUTIVE GAMES.

sports

 Jockey Willie Shoemaker rode 485 winners, well above the record. **Robert H. McDaniel** broke records as trainer of more than 200 winners.

BEN HOGAN SCORED BIG SUCCESSES IN THE U.S. AND BRITISH OPENS, AND HE WAS COMPARED WITH BOBBY JONES, THE GOLFING GREAT OF AN EARLIER GENERATION.

Academy Award winners for 1953 films: Best Picture was **From Here to Eternity.** Other nominees were *Julius Caesar, The Robe, Roman Holiday,* and *Shane.* **Fred Zinnemann** took Best Director honors for *From Here to Eternity.* He won out over George Stevens, Charles Walters, Billy Wilder, and William Wyler. **William Holden** was named Best Actor for his role in *Stalag 17.* The other nominees were Marlon Brando, Richard Burton, Montgomery Clift, and Burt Lancaster. Best Actress winner was **Audrey Hepburn,** star of *Roman Holiday.* Her competition consisted of Leslie Caron *(Lili),* Ava Gardner *(Mogambo),* Deborah Kerr *(From Here to Eternity),* and Maggie McNamara *(The Moon Is Blue).* **Frank Sinatra** won the Best Supporting Actor Oscar for his performance in *From Here to Eternity.* **Donna Reed,** also in *Eternity,* won as Best Supporting Actress.

box-office champs

1. **The Robe** ($20–30 million)
2. **From Here to Eternity** ($12.5 million)
3. **Shane** ($8 million)
4. **How to Marry a Millionaire** ($7.5 million)
5. **Peter Pan** ($7 million)
6. **Hans Christian Andersen** ($6 million)
7. **House of Wax** ($5.5 million)
8. **Mogambo** ($5.2 million)
9. **Gentlemen Prefer Blondes** ($5.1 million)
10. **Moulin Rouge** ($5 million)

top ten box-office actors

1. Gary Cooper
2. Dean Martin & Jerry Lewis
3. John Wayne
4. Alan Ladd
5. Bing Crosby
6. Marilyn Monroe
7. James Stewart
8. Bob Hope
9. Susan Hayward
10. Randolph Scott

By mid-1953, more than 40 percent of movies released were in color.

movies

WEEKLY ATTENDANCE AT THEATERS WAS ABOUT 46 MILLION. THEATER GROSSES WERE ESTIMATED AT AN ANNUAL RATE OF $1.2 BILLION.

Various wide-screen and 3-D processes tended to boost attendance. Among the 3-D pictures released were *House of Wax, Bwana Devil, It Came from Outer Space,* and *Inferno.*

'53

Automatic transmissions had gained fast acceptance; in 1953, more than 50 percent of cars had some kind of automatic shift. Power steering began to appear in the lower-priced lines. One car offered a power seat adjuster. Air-conditioning,

There was a color explosion in cars—bright reds, browns, ivories, greens, and blues.

cars

introduced in 1952, was extended to several models in 1953. Although for many years black was the dominant color in cars, now it was used in only one car out of eight.

BRINGS THE OUTDOORS INDOORS—Moving walls of glass give new dimensions to the homes of today. Lincoln mirrors this trend with 3,721 square inches of cool sea-tint* visibility—vision that includes both front fenders. Think of what that means when parking, or when you need to see close up.

DAY'S PUSH-BUTTON MAGIC—like television—makes life easier, more comfortable. In Lincoln, controls open windows electrically,* provide quick heat and ventilation, automatically adjust car's speed to driving needs (dual range HYDRA-MATIC Transmission as standard equipment). And never before such easy handling, with an exclusive new ball joint front suspension system, first on a U.S. production car.

LINCOLN

captures the beautiful ease of modern living

*Electric window operation, sea-tint glass and white side-wall tires optional at extra cost. Standard equipment, accessories, and trim illustrated are subject to change without notice.

No matter what the luxury—be comfortable. That is the mood today. In homes there are *fewer* rooms for show, *more* rooms that welcome people, living rooms made for *living*. You see it all around you in your home... but what about the car in your garage?

Do you see a pompous automobile? Or do you see the clean-lined beauty of the one fine car designed for this new way of life—Lincoln for 1952?

For this year's Lincoln is the car that lets you take modern living with you. Luxurious, yes... probably the most carefully and finely crafted car of our time. But, for all its luxury, it is magnificently functional. For all its roominess, it is quick and eager—with a completely new overhead valve V-8 engine, winner in its field in the Mobilgas Economy Run.

You can make your driving as modern as your living. First—at your Lincoln dealer's showroom, inspect the new Lincoln Cosmopolitan and Capri. Then—drive *the one fine car deliberately designed for modern living.*

LINCOLN DIVISION · FORD MOTOR COMPANY

The mood was sleek, slender, and elegant combined with a gamine quality—both young and sophisticated. Hemlines, waistlines, and hairlines all grew shorter. Even sports clothes

The "Italian" haircut, with carefully "casual" tendrils around the face, superseded the shorter, curlier **"poodle cut."**

fashion

the mood was sleek, slender, and elegant

were elegant and ultra-feminine. Slacks and at-home pants tapered to the ankle. The British coronation helped make jewel colors popular. Accessories were: stoles of every material and description, very bare shoes and Italian mules, large hoop earrings, and, of course, wonderful hats. There were tiny hats that perched on heads, turbans, pillboxes, toques, and sailor hats.

Fashion experts noted the beginning of a revival of "male plumage." Prominent designers of women's wear entered the field of men's design. Sports clothes of colorful silks and cottons were very popular with men. Silk suits for men were a widespread summer fashion.

Harmau

GEOFFREY

final factoid

With the move to the suburbs, many families became deeply involved with lawn care. One 1953 ad with master golfer Sam Snead as spokesman promoted a huge variety of Toro power mowers. The new electric model was $69.95.

archive photos: pages 1, 6, 7, 11, 13, 14, 25, inside back cover.

associated press: pages 5,.10, 16.

photofest : insede front cover, pages 2, 3, 7, 8, 9, 18, 19.

original photography:
beth phillips: pages 13, 21, 23.

album cover:
courtesy of bob george/
the archive of contemporary music: page 13

photo research:
alice albert

coordination:
rustyn birch

design:
carol bokuniewicz design
mutsumi hyuga

'53